Alfred

Produced by
Alfred Music Publishing Co., Inc.
P.O. Box 10003
Van Nuys, CA 91410-0003
alfred.com

Printed in USA.

ISBN-10: 0-7390-8296-5
ISBN-13: 978-0-7390-8296-6

THE LEGEND OF ZELDA™ Series

for Piano

INTERMEDIATE-ADVANCED EDITION

CONTENTS

The Legend of Zelda™

Title Theme 4

Main Theme 6

Tri-Force Fanfare 84

Correct Solution 84

Whistle of Warp 84

Zelda II™: The Adventure of Link™

Title Theme 8

Palace Music 10

The Legend of Zelda™: A Link to the Past™

Title Screen 12

Hyrule Castle Music 13

Main Theme 16

The Dark World 18

The Legend of Zelda™: Link's Awakening™

Main Theme 20

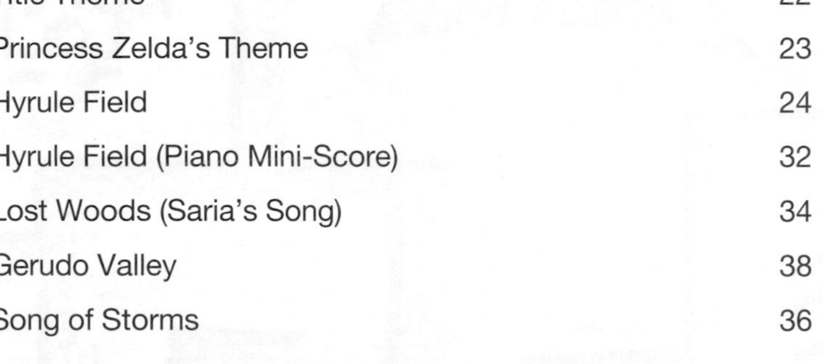

The Legend of Zelda™: Ocarina of Time™

Title Theme 22
Princess Zelda's Theme 23
Hyrule Field 24
Hyrule Field (Piano Mini-Score) 32
Lost Woods (Saria's Song) 34
Gerudo Valley 38
Song of Storms 36

The Legend of Zelda™: Majora's Mask™

Prelude of Majora's Mask 41
Termina Field 45

The Legend of Zelda™: The Wind Waker™

Main Theme 48
Dragon Roost Island 50
Ocean Theme 56
Molgera 53

The Legend of Zelda™: Four Swords Adventures

Village of the Blue Maiden Restored 60
Field Theme 62

The Legend of Zelda™: Twilight Princess

Hyrule Field Main Theme 66
Hidden Village 70
Midna's Lament 72

The Legend of Zelda™: Phantom Hourglass

Ciela's Parting Words 74

The Legend of Zelda™: Spirit Tracks

Title Theme 76
Field Theme 78
Train Travel (Main Theme) 80

THE LEGEND OF ZELDA™: TITLE THEME

Piano arrangement by SHINOBU AMAYAKE
Music supervision by NINTENDO

Composed by KOJI KONDO

(Original Key : B♭)

C
f
F.O.

THE LEGEND OF ZELDA™: MAIN THEME

Piano arrangement by SHINOBU AMAYAKE
Music supervision by NINTENDO

Composed by KOJI KONDO

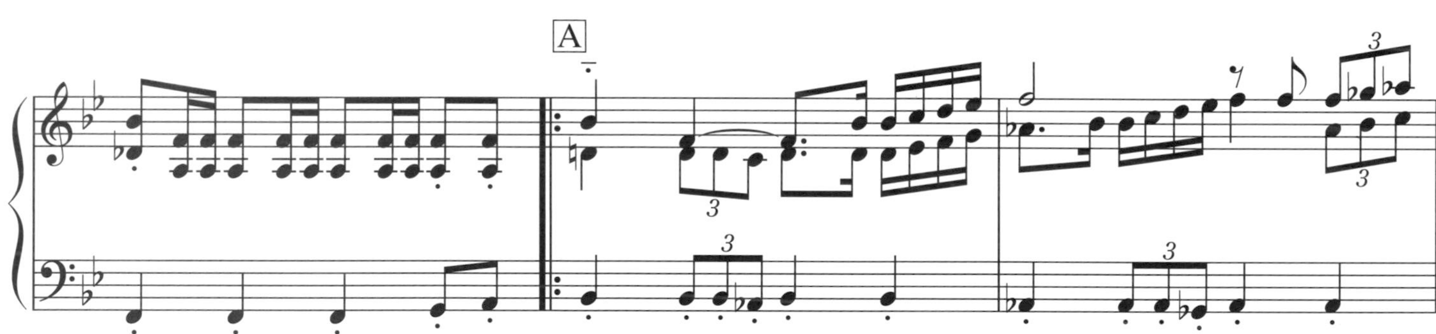

B
F.O.

ZELDA II™: The Adventure of Link™
TITLE THEME

Piano arrangement by SHINOBU AMAYAKE
Music supervision by NINTENDO

Composed by AKITO NAKATSUKA

(Original Key : F)

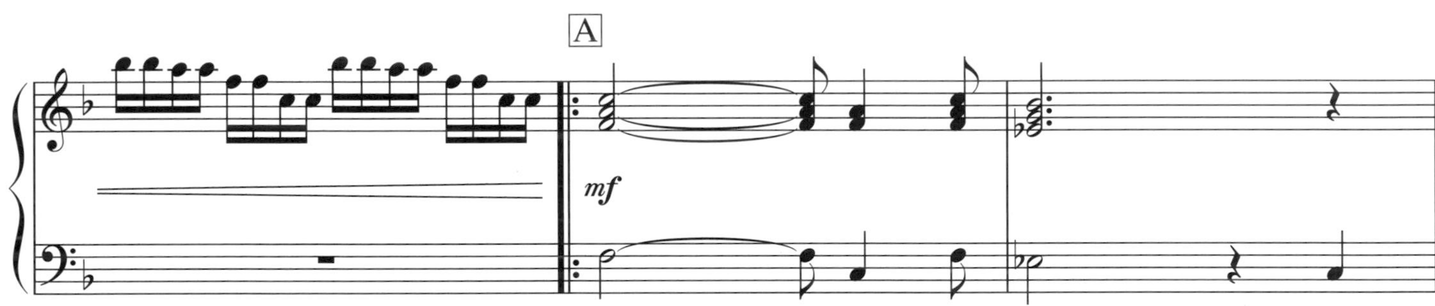

B
C
F.O.

ZELDA II™: The Adventure of Link™
PALACE MUSIC

Piano arrangement by SHINOBU AMAYAKE
Music supervision by NINTENDO

Composed by AKITO NAKATSUKA

(Original Key : Gm)

C
2.
f
D
mf
D.S.&F.O.

THE LEGEND OF ZELDA™: A Link to the Past™

TITLE SCREEN

Piano arrangement by SHINOBU AMAYAKE
Music supervision by NINTENDO

Composed by KOJI KONDO

(Original Key : A♭)

THE LEGEND OF ZELDA™: A Link to the Past™

HYRULE CASTLE MUSIC

Piano arrangement by SHINOBU AMAYAKE
Music supervision by NINTENDO

Composed by KOJI KONDO

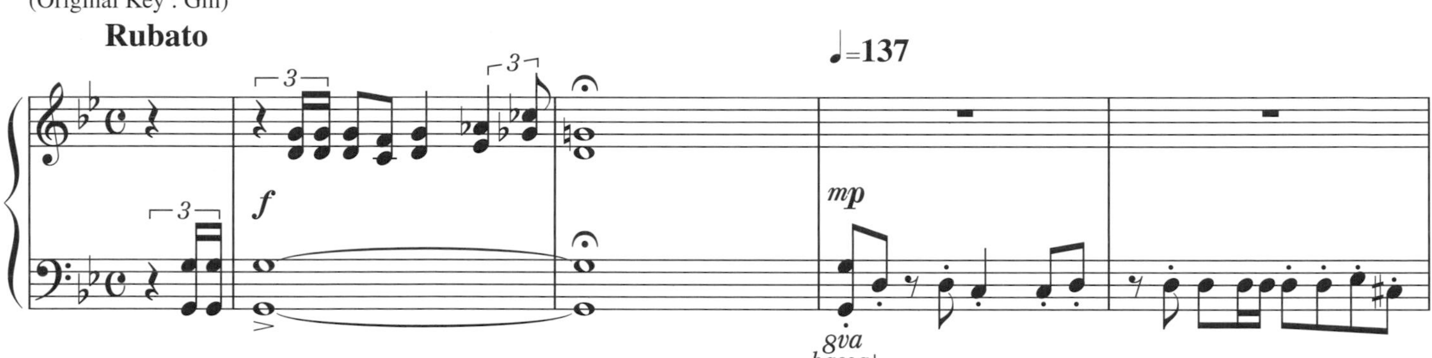

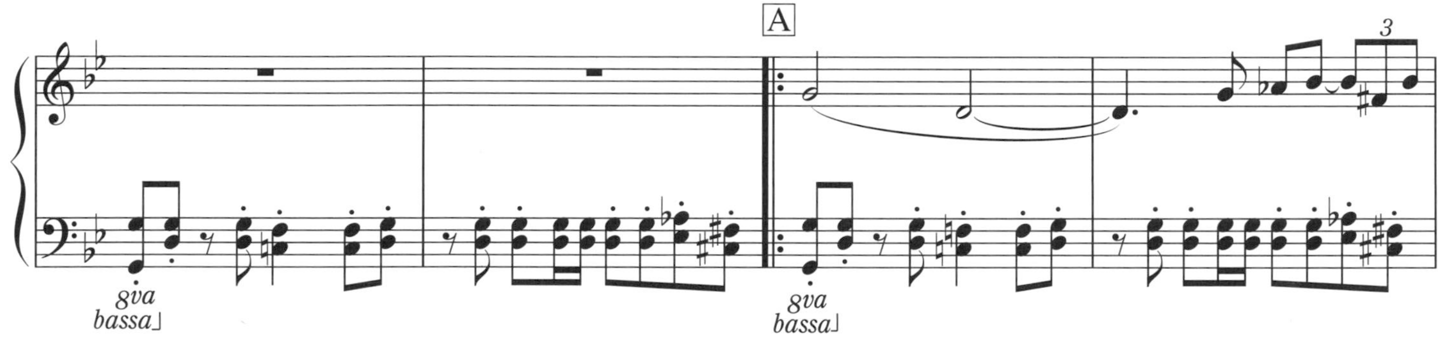

8va bassa
8va bassa
B
mf
f
8va bassa
8va bassa
mf
8va bassa
(8va bassa)
f

C
mp
D
mf
8va bassa
(8va bassa)
(8va bassa)
mp
8va bassa
F.O.

THE LEGEND OF ZELDA™: A Link to the Past™

MAIN THEME

Piano arrangement by SHINOBU AMAYAKE
Music supervision by NINTENDO

Composed by KOJI KONDO

(Original Key : B♭)

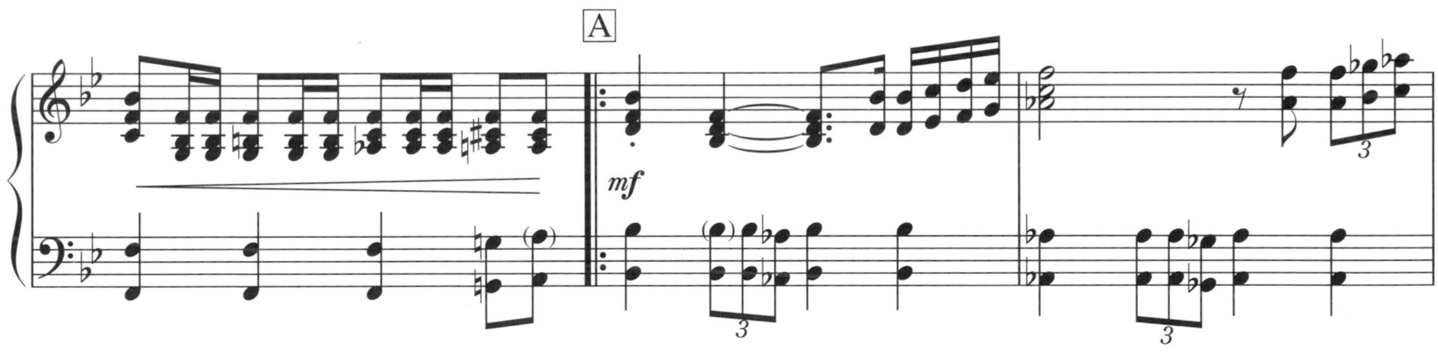

B
mf
f
Ped.
mf
Ped.
F.O.

THE LEGEND OF ZELDA™: A Link to the Past™

THE DARK WORLD

Piano arrangement by SHINOBU AMAYAKE
Music supervision by NINTENDO

Composed by KOJI KONDO

(Original Key : Cm)

C
mp
mf
f
D.C.& F.O.

THE LEGEND OF ZELDA™: *Link's Awakening*™

MAIN THEME

Piano arrangement by SHINOBU AMAYAKE
Music supervision by NINTENDO

Composed by KOJI KONDO and KOZUE ISHIKAWA

(Original Key : G)

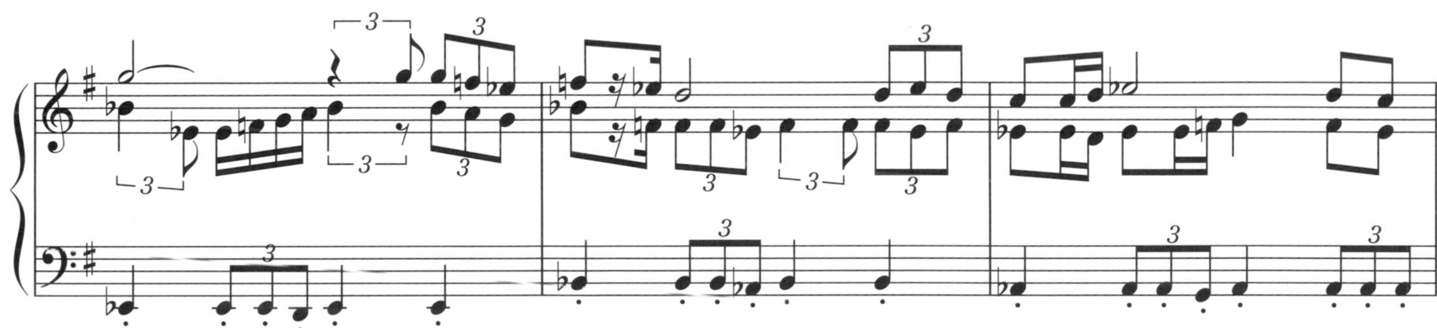

B
C
l.h.
f
F.O.

THE LEGEND OF ZELDA™: Ocarina of Time™
TITLE THEME

Piano arrangement by SHINOBU AMAYAKE
Music supervision by NINTENDO

Composed by KOJI KONDO

(Original Key : C)

♩=74

mp

A

B

mf

mp

F.O.

THE LEGEND OF ZELDA™: Ocarina of Time™

PRINCESS ZELDA'S THEME

(Original Key : Em)

Composed by KOJI KONDO
Piano arrangement by SHINOBU AMAYAKE
Music supervision by NINTENDO

♩=110

A

mp

rit.

B *a tempo*

8va

mf

F.O.

THE LEGEND OF ZELDA™: Ocarina of Time™

HYRULE FIELD

Piano arrangement by SHINOBU AMAYAKE
Music supervision by NINTENDO

Composed by KOJI KONDO

(Original Key : G)

♩=150

f sf mp mf

A

B

8va

mf
8va
3
C
mf
D
mp
Ped.
Ped.
Ped.
Ped.
E

F
G
mf
mp
H

I
mf
J
mf

mp
mf
K
f
L
mf

M

mf

N

f *mf*

♩=138
P
mp
3
Q
p
Ped.
l.h.
mf
R

S
mp
Ped.
T
♩=150
mf
U
mp
D.S.& F.O.

THE LEGEND OF ZELDA™: Ocarina of Time™
HYRULE FIELD (PIANO MINI-SCORE)

Composed by KOJI KONDO
Piano arrangement by SHINOBU AMAYAKE
Music supervision by NINTENDO

K
L
M
N
O
P
Q
R
S
T
U
♩=138
♩=150
mp
mf
f
p
l.h.
D.S.& F.O.

THE LEGEND OF ZELDA™: *Ocarina of Time™*

LOST WOODS (SARIA'S SONG)

Piano arrangement by SHINOBU AMAYAKE
Music supervision by NINTENDO

Composed by KOJI KONDO

(Original Key : C)

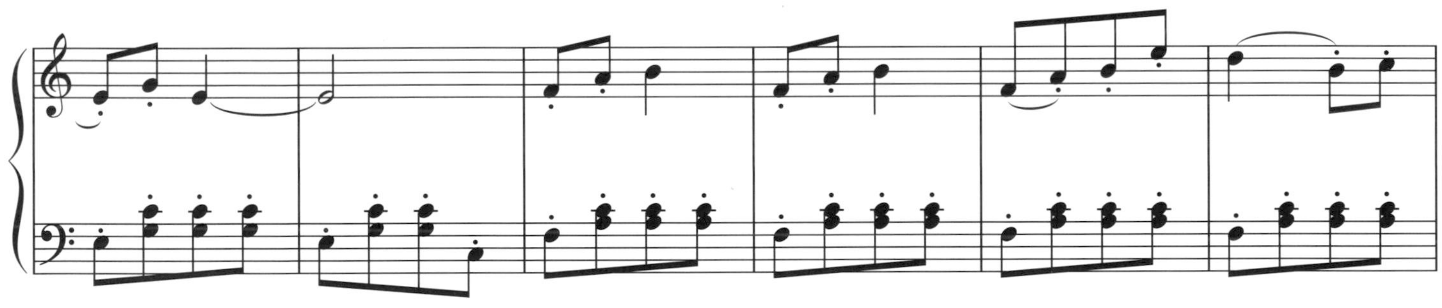

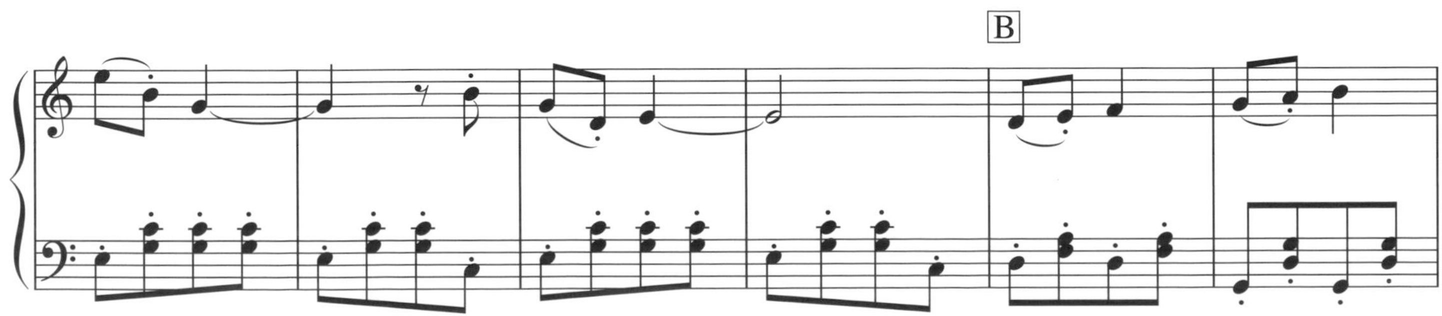

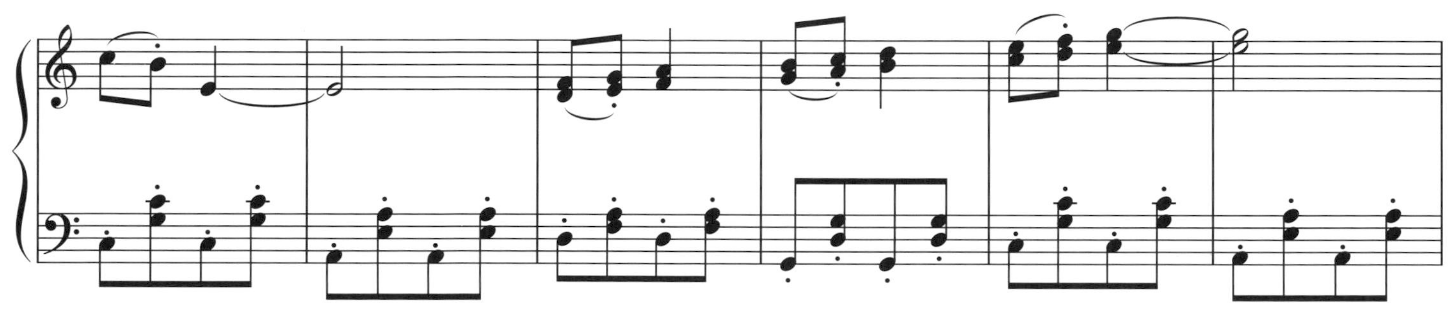

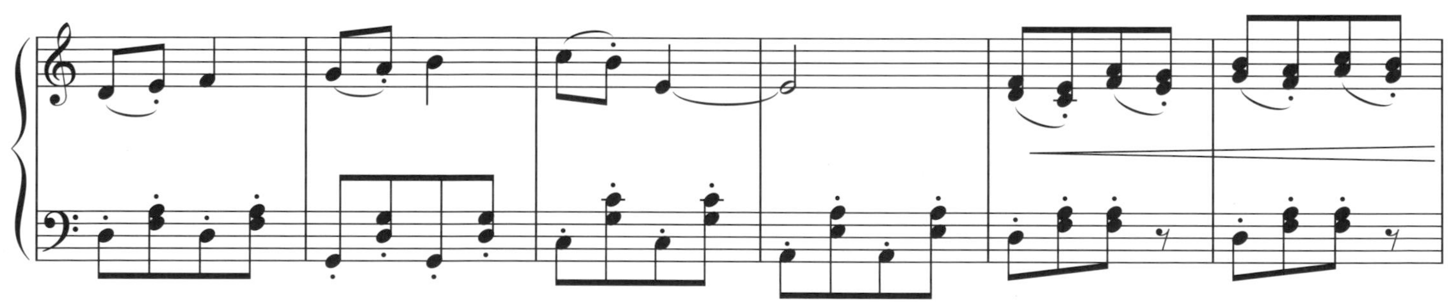

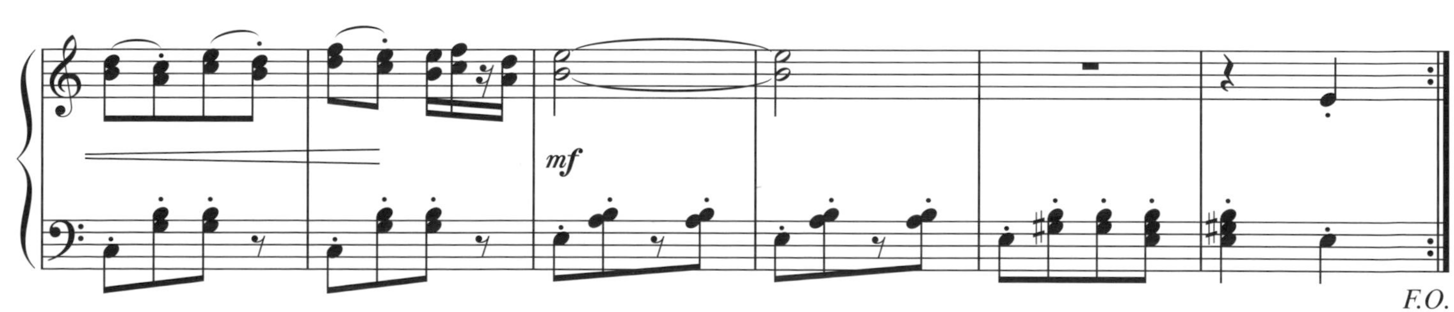

F.O.

THE LEGEND OF ZELDA™: *Ocarina of Time*™

SONG OF STORMS

Piano arrangement by SHINOBU AMAYAKE
Music supervision by NINTENDO

Composed by KOJI KONDO

(Original Key : Dm)

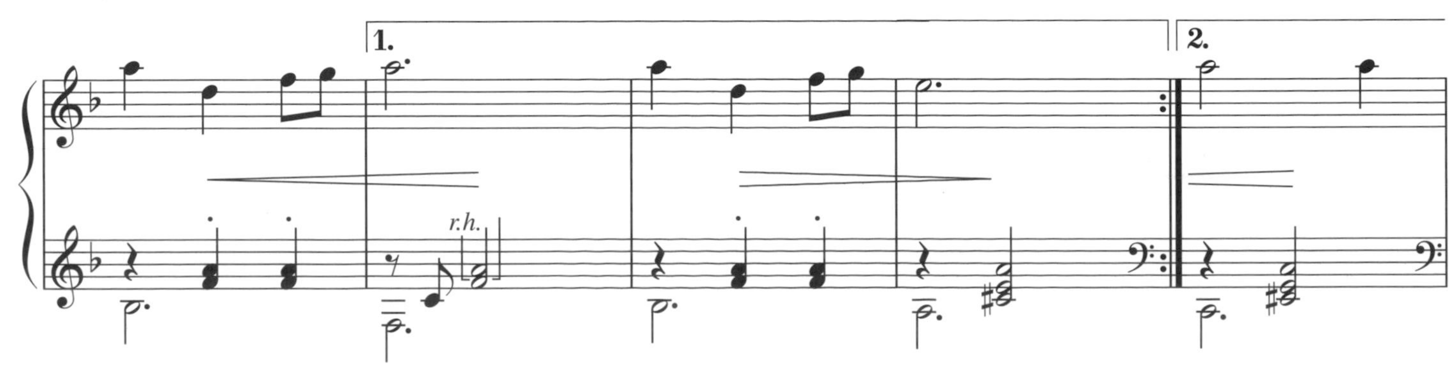

B
mp
C
r.h.
1.
2.
mp
D.S.& F.O.

THE LEGEND OF ZELDA™: Ocarina of Time™
GERUDO VALLEY

Piano arrangement by SHINOBU AMAYAKE
Music supervision by NINTENDO

Composed by KOJI KONDO

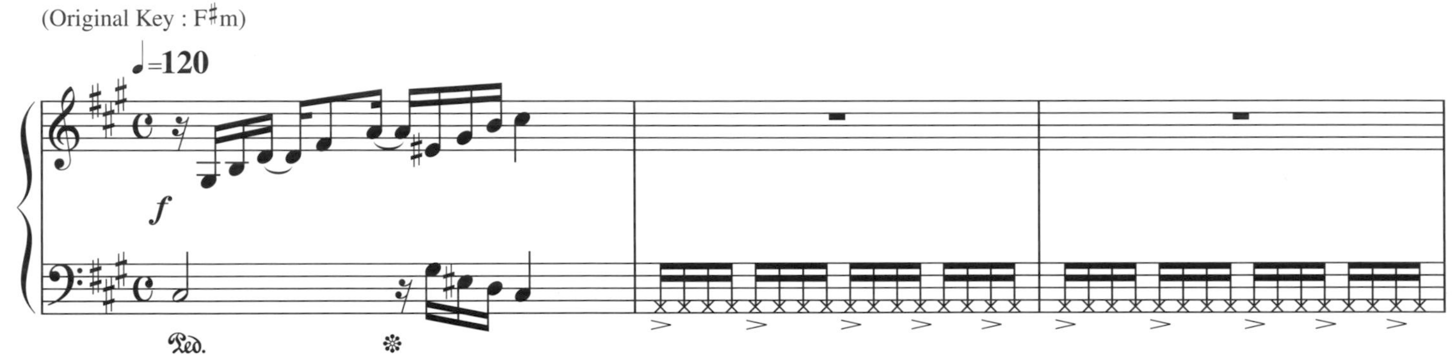

p

A

mp

1.

2.

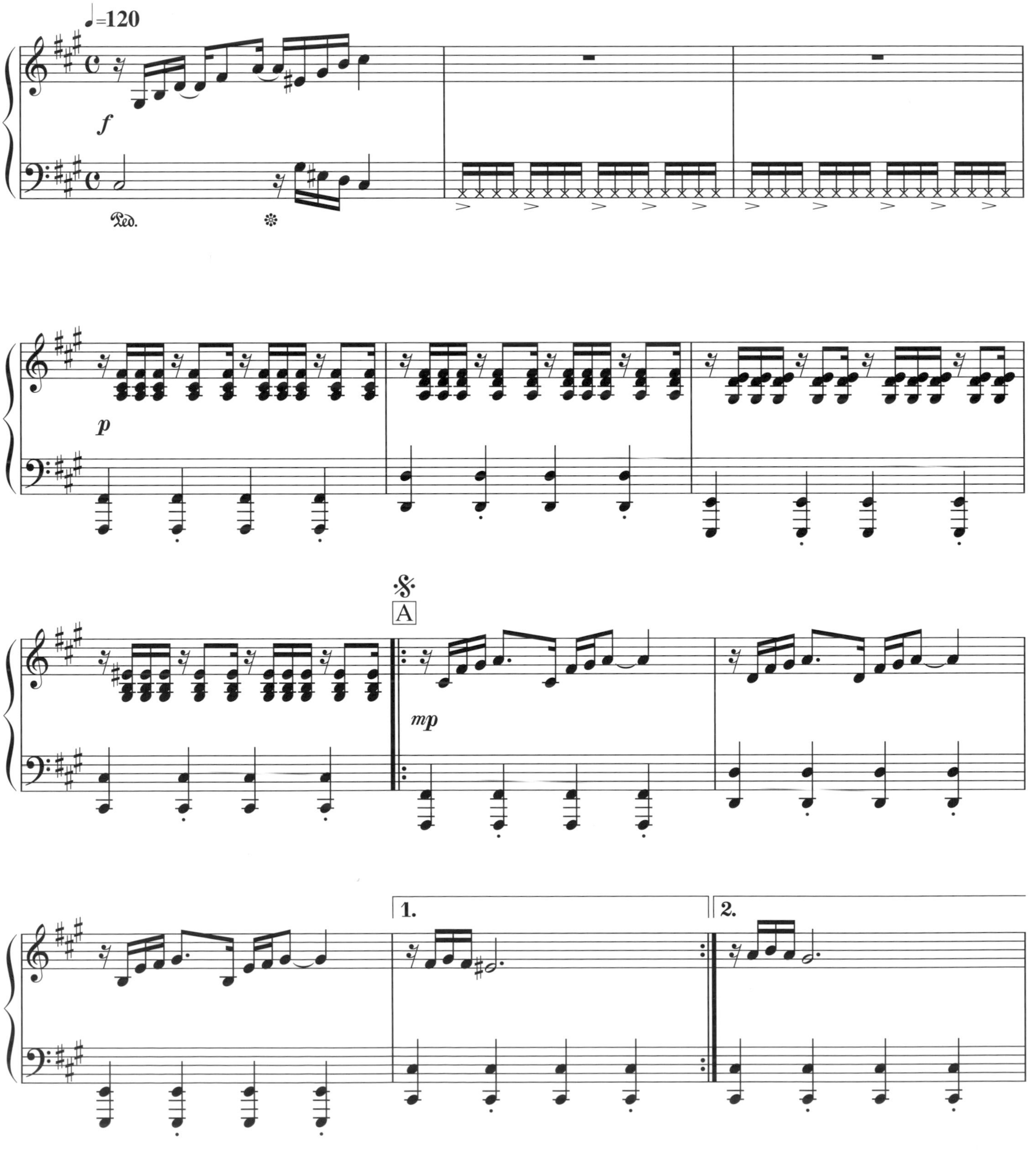

B
C

D
mf
p
D.S.&F.O.

THE LEGEND OF ZELDA™: Majora's Mask™
PRELUDE OF MAJORA'S MASK

Piano arrangement by SHINOBU AMAYAKE
Music supervision by NINTENDO

Composed by KOJI KONDO

(Original Key : D)

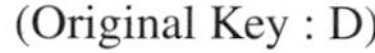

B
1.
C
mf

l.h.
2.
pp
mf
pp
D
f
r.h.

THE LEGEND OF
ZELDA®
MAJORA'S MASK™

THE LEGEND OF ZELDA™: Majora's Mask™
TERMINA FIELD

Piano arrangement by SHINOBU AMAYAKE
Music supervision by NINTENDO

Composed by KOJI KONDO

(Original Key : G)

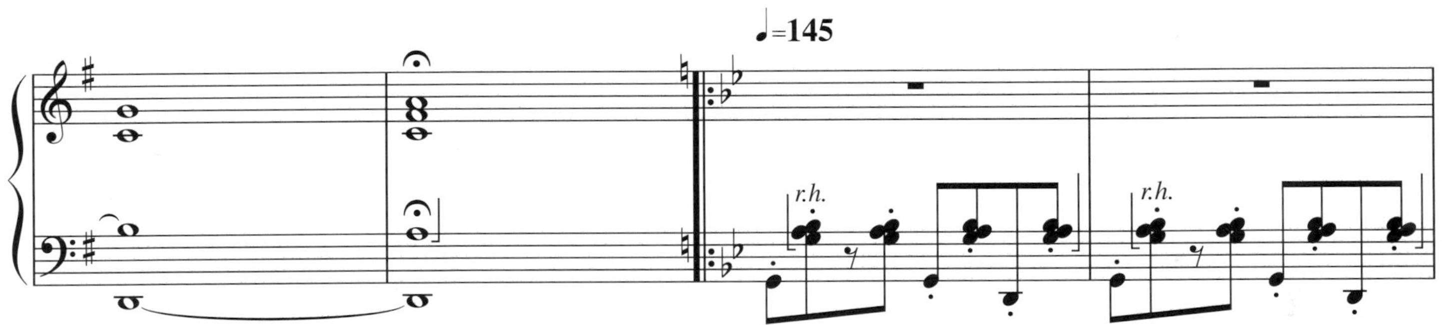

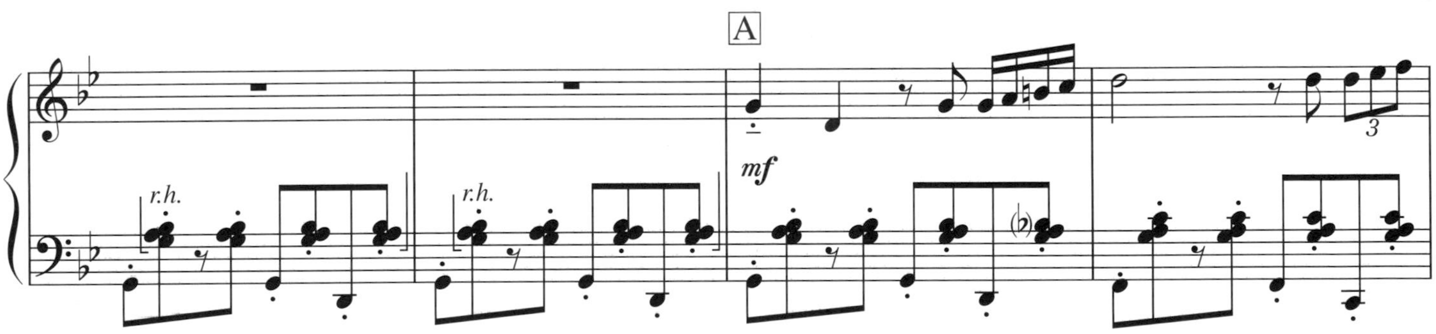

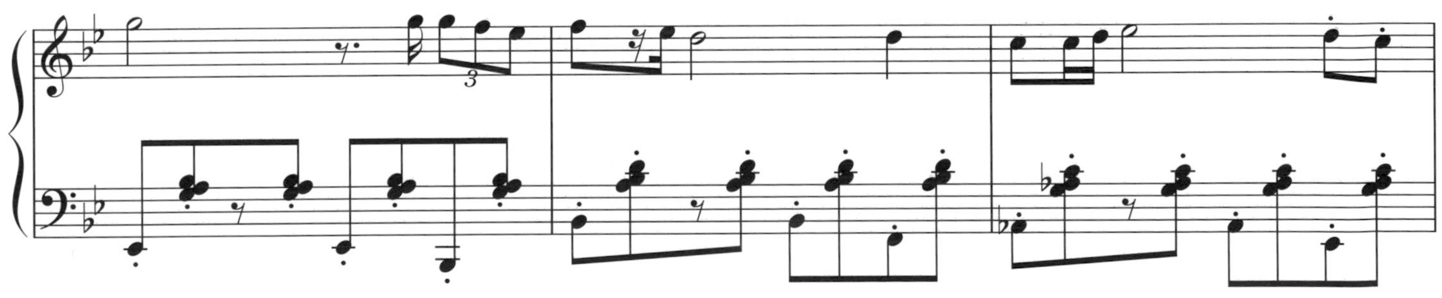

B
mf
3
f

C
mf
3
3
f
F.O.

THE LEGEND OF ZELDA™: The Wind Waker™

MAIN THEME

Piano arrangement by SHINOBU AMAYAKE
Music supervision by NINTENDO

Composed by KENTA NAGATA

(Original Key : D♭)

C
1.
2.
D
mp
D.S.& F.O.

THE LEGEND OF ZELDA™: The Wind Waker™
DRAGON ROOST ISLAND

Piano arrangement by SHINOBU AMAYAKE
Music supervision by NINTENDO

Composed by KENTA NAGATA

(Original Key :Gm)

♩=172

f

mf

A

B
mf
C
f

D
mf
E
f
F.O.

THE LEGEND OF ZELDA™: The Wind Waker™
MOLGERA

Piano arrangement by SHINOBU AMAYAKE
Music supervision by NINTENDO

Composed by HAJIME WAKAI

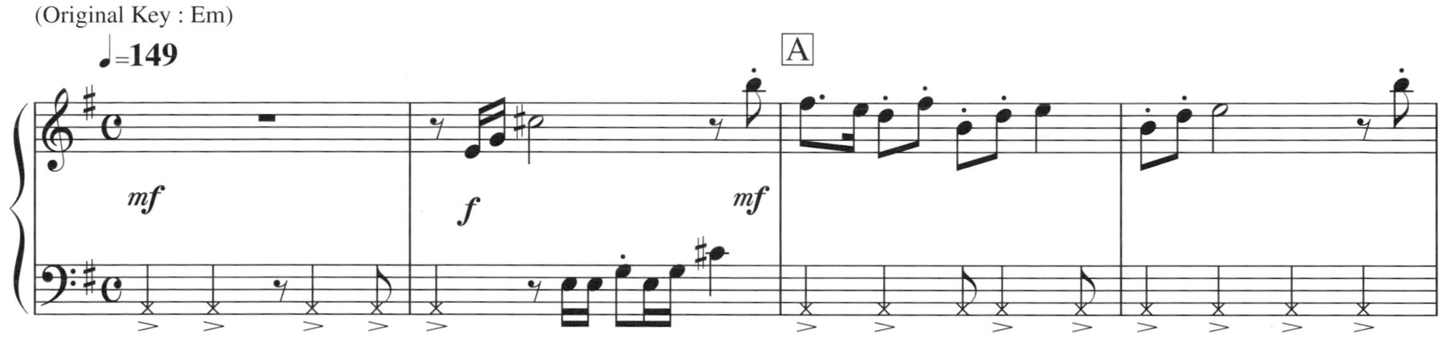

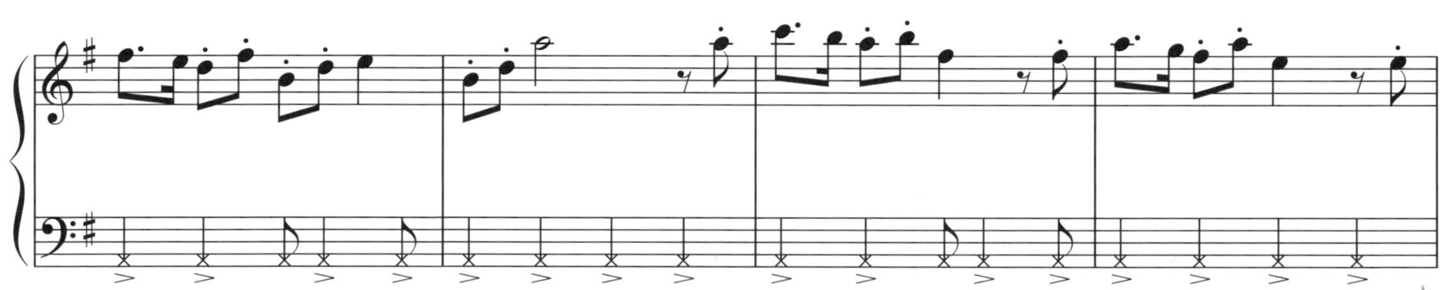

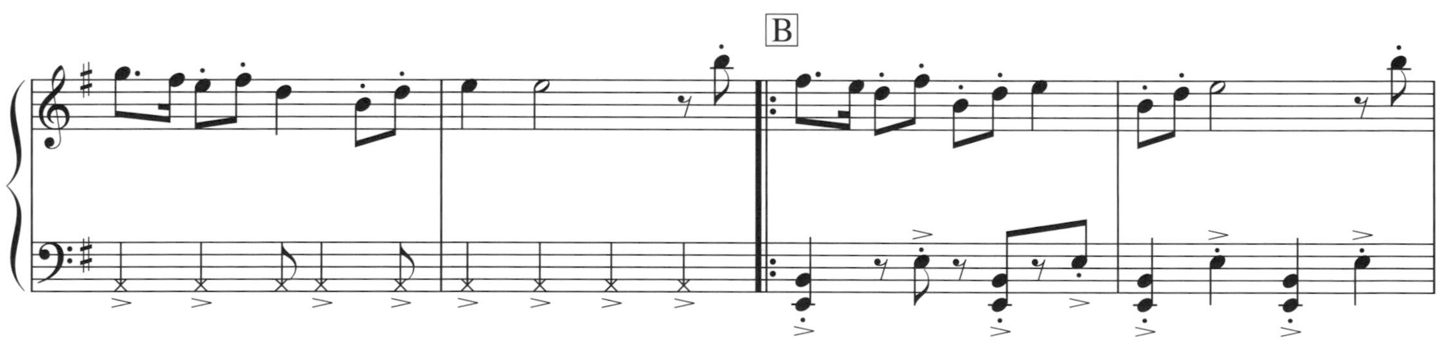

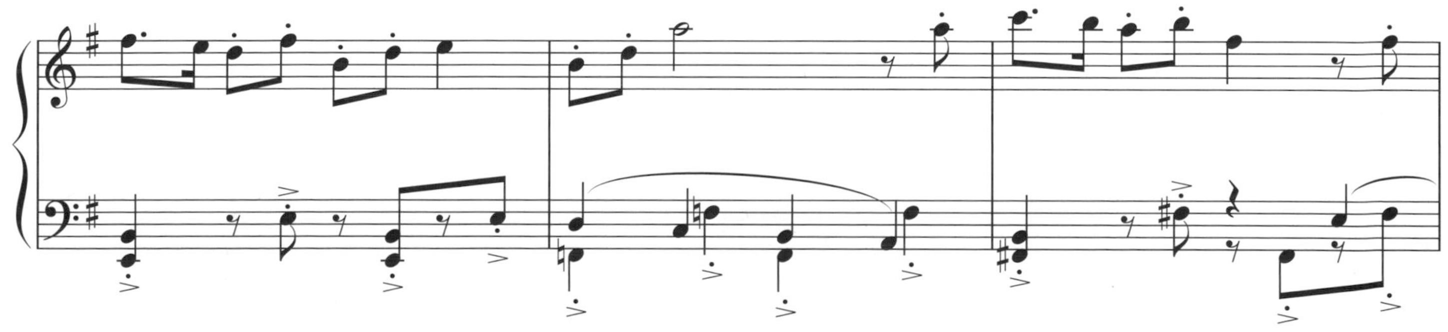

C
3
D

f
E
sf
p
f
mf
F
F.O.

THE LEGEND OF ZELDA™: The Wind Waker™

OCEAN THEME

Piano arrangement by SHINOBU AMAYAKE
Music supervision by NINTENDO

Composed by KENTA NAGATA

(Original Key : D)

1.
2.

B
mf
C
mf
1.

2.
D
mf
D.S. & F.O.

THE LEGEND OF ZELDA™: Four Swords Adventures

VILLAGE OF THE BLUE MAIDEN RESTORED

Piano arrangement by SHINOBU AMAYAKE
Music supervision by NINTENDO

Composed by KOJI KONDO and ASUKA OHTA

(Original Key : B♭)

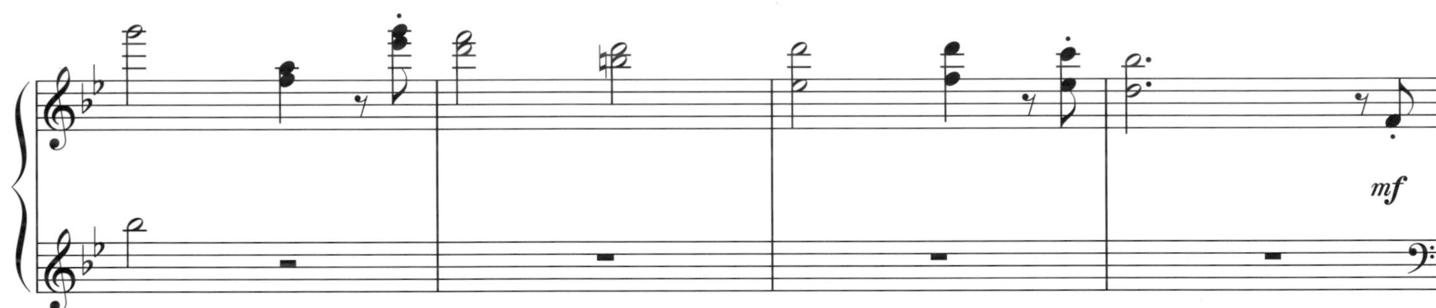

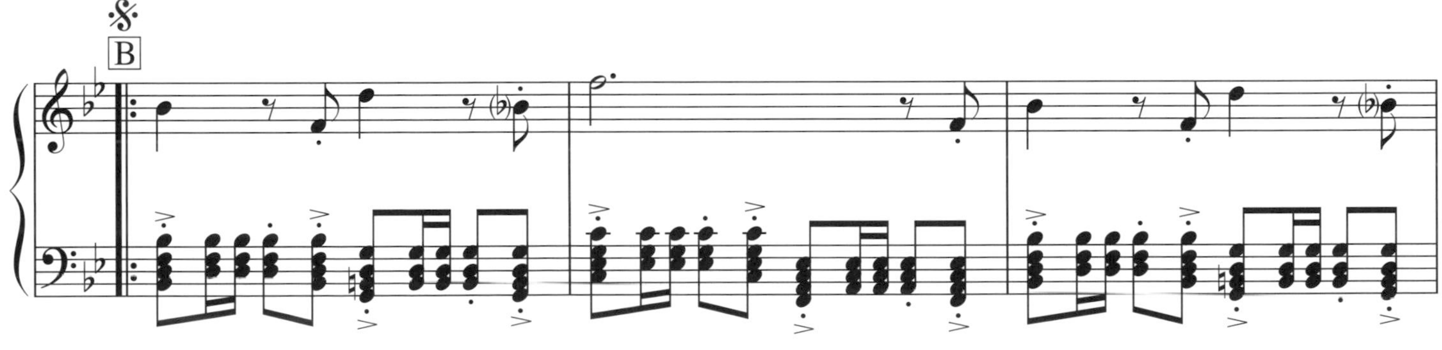

1.
C
f
2.
D
mp
mf
D.S.& F.O.

THE LEGEND OF ZELDA™: Four Swords Adventures

FIELD THEME

Piano arrangement by SHINOBU AMAYAKE
Music supervision by NINTENDO

Composed by ASUKA OHTA

(Original Key : G)

♩=144

mf r.h.

A

(mf)

tr

3

B
3
f
C
mp
8va

D
mf
f
F.O.

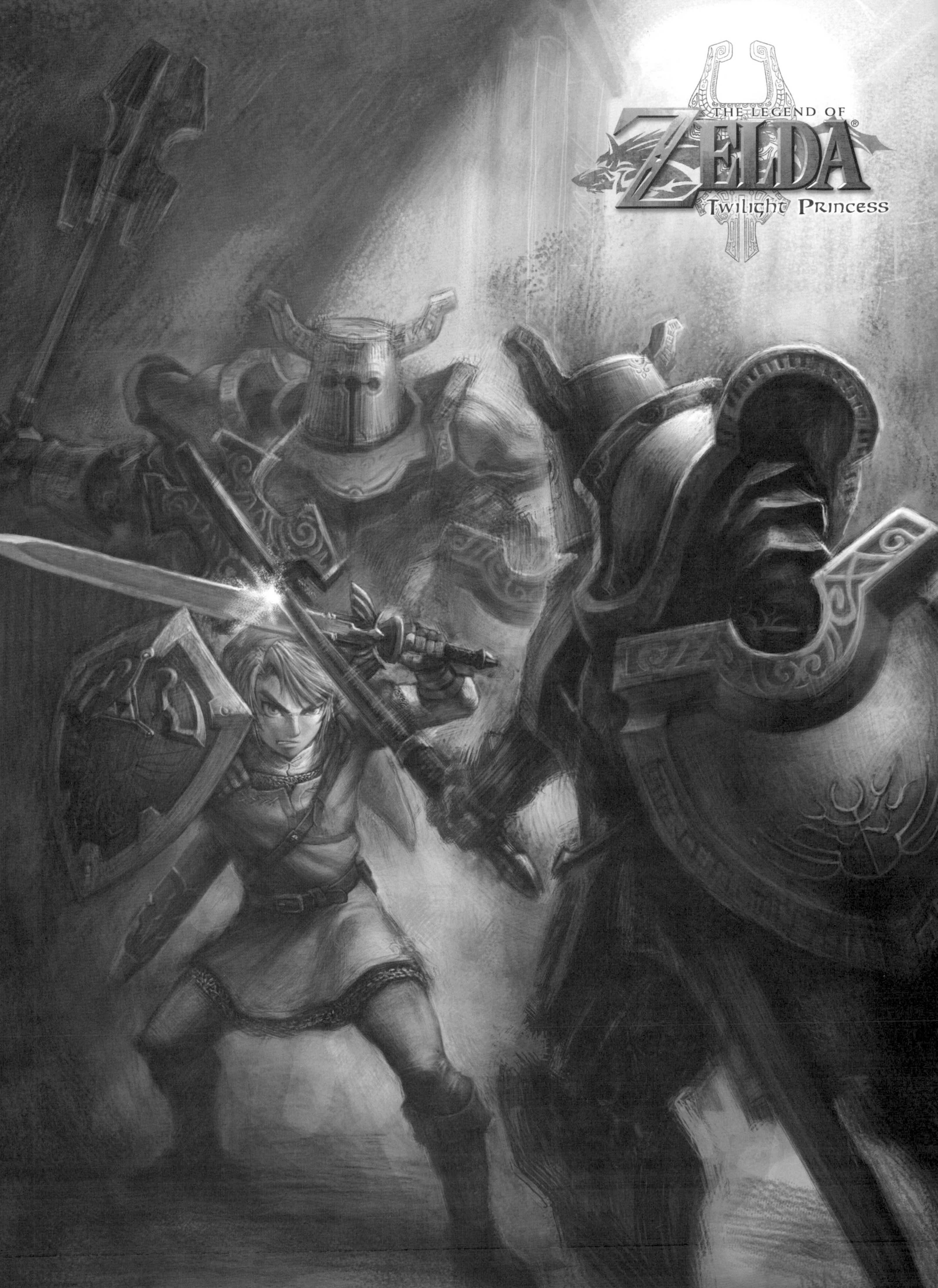
THE LEGEND OF
ZELDA
Twilight Princess

THE LEGEND OF ZELDA™: Twilight Princess

HYRULE FIELD MAIN THEME

Piano arrangement by SHINOBU AMAYAKE
Music supervision by NINTENDO

Composed by TORU MINEGISHI

(Original Key : Em)

B
f
C
3
D
Ped.

3
simile
E
mf
Ped.
Ped.
Ped.
simile
f

F
G
r.h.
r.h.
r.h.
D.S.& F.O.

THE LEGEND OF ZELDA™: Twilight Princess
HIDDEN VILLAGE

Piano arrangement by SHINOBU AMAYAKE
Music supervision by NINTENDO

Composed by TORU MINEGISHI

(Original Key : Bm)

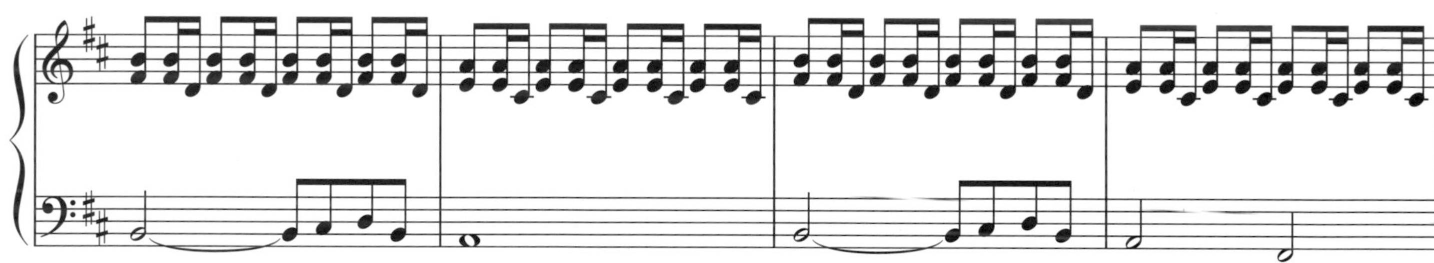

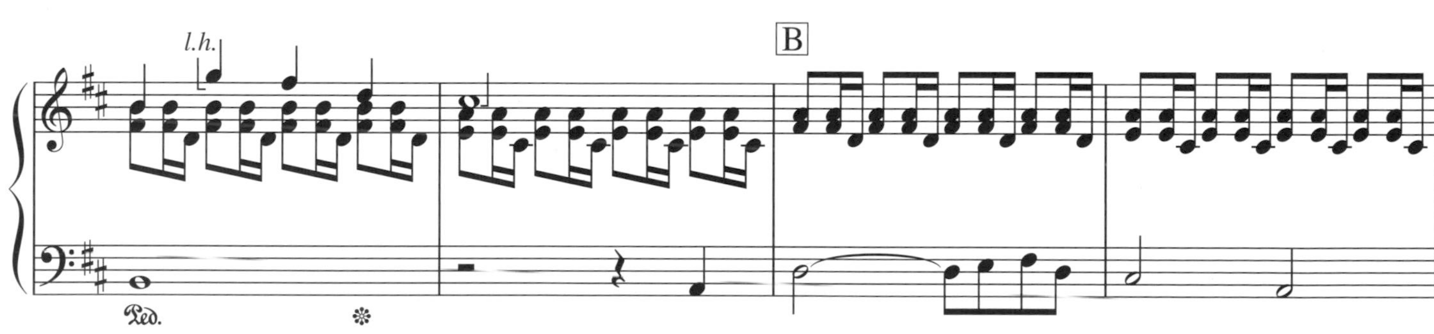

l.h.
C
Ped.
D
f
mf
F.O.

THE LEGEND OF ZELDA™: *Twilight Princess*
MIDNA'S LAMENT

Piano arrangement by SHINOBU AMAYAKE
Music supervision by NINTENDO

Composed by TORU MINEGISHI

(Original Key : Dm)

♩=132

mp *r.h.* *r.h.* *r.h.*

Ped. * Ped. * Ped. *

A

(*mp*)

Ped. * *simile*

8va

B

8va

1.

C

mf

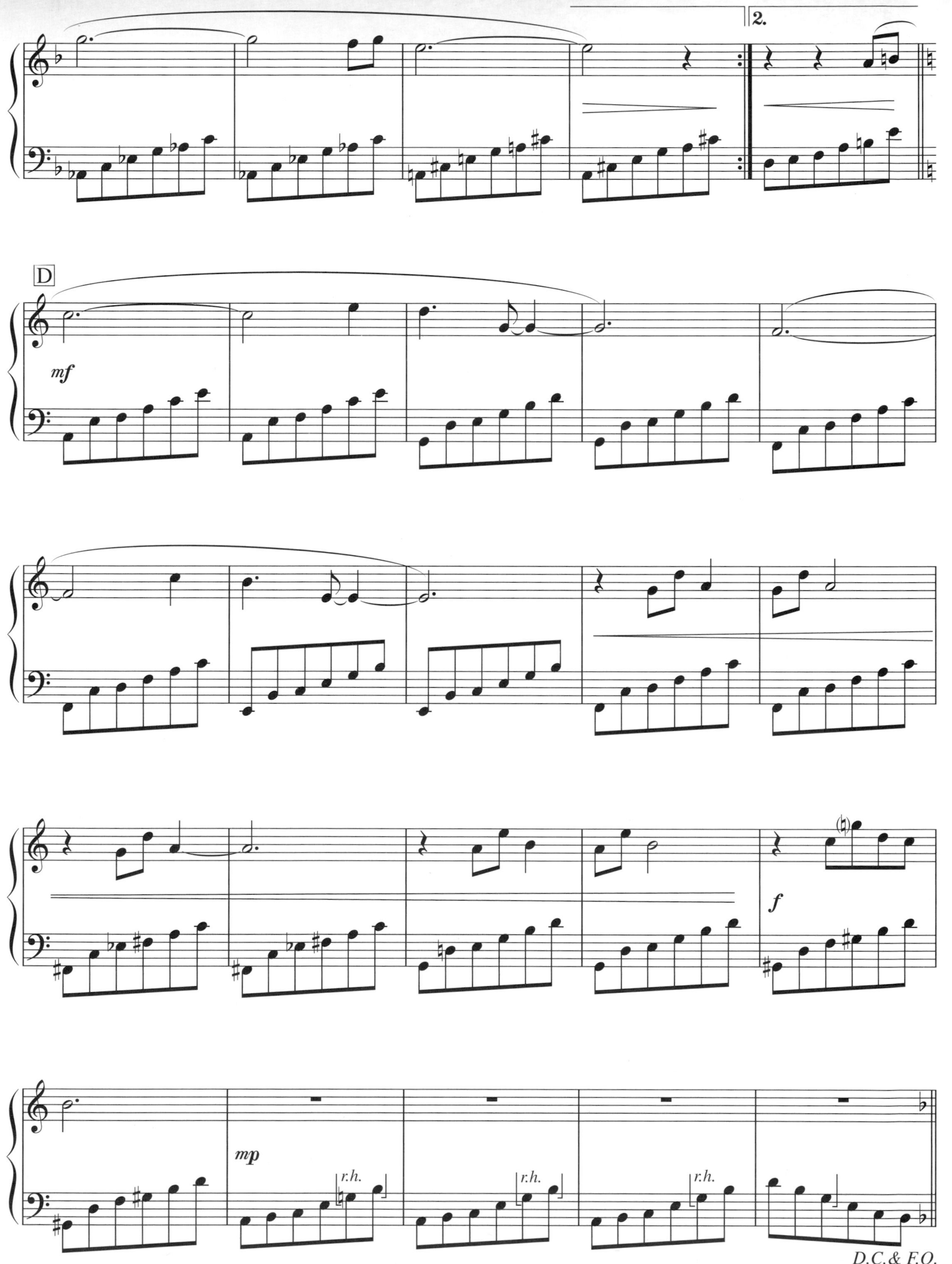
2.
D
mf
f
mp
r.h.
r.h.
r.h.
D.C.& F.O.

THE LEGEND OF ZELDA™: Phantom Hourglass

CIELA'S PARTING WORDS

Piano arrangement by SHINOBU AMAYAKE
Music supervision by NINTENDO

Composed by KOJI KONDO and TORU MINEGISHI

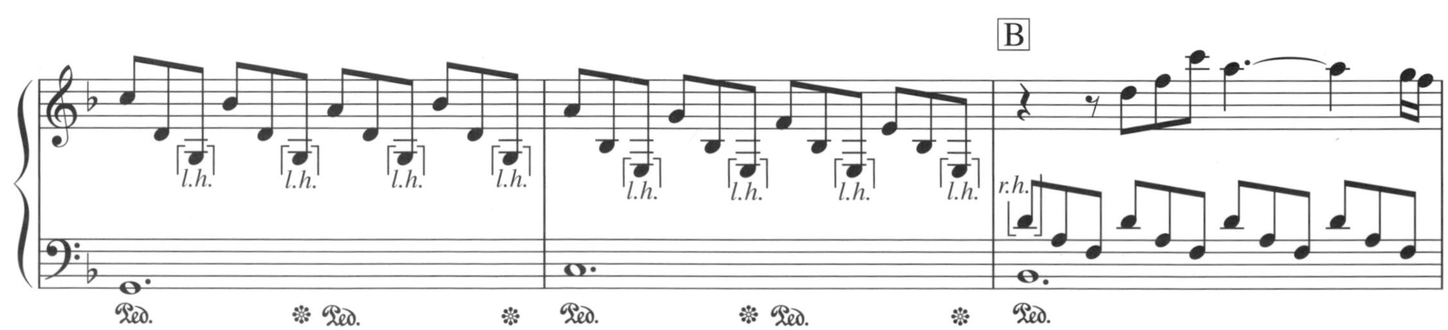

r.h.
r.h.
r.h.
r.h.
Ped.
Ped.
Ped.
Ped.
Ped.
Ped.

r.h.
Ped.
Ped.
Ped.

C
mp
F.O.
Ped.
Ped.
Ped.
Ped.
Ped.
Ped.

THE LEGEND OF ZELDA™:
Spirit Tracks

TITLE THEME

Piano arrangement by SHINOBU AMAYAKE
Music supervision by NINTENDO

Composed by TORU MINEGISHI

(Original Key : A)

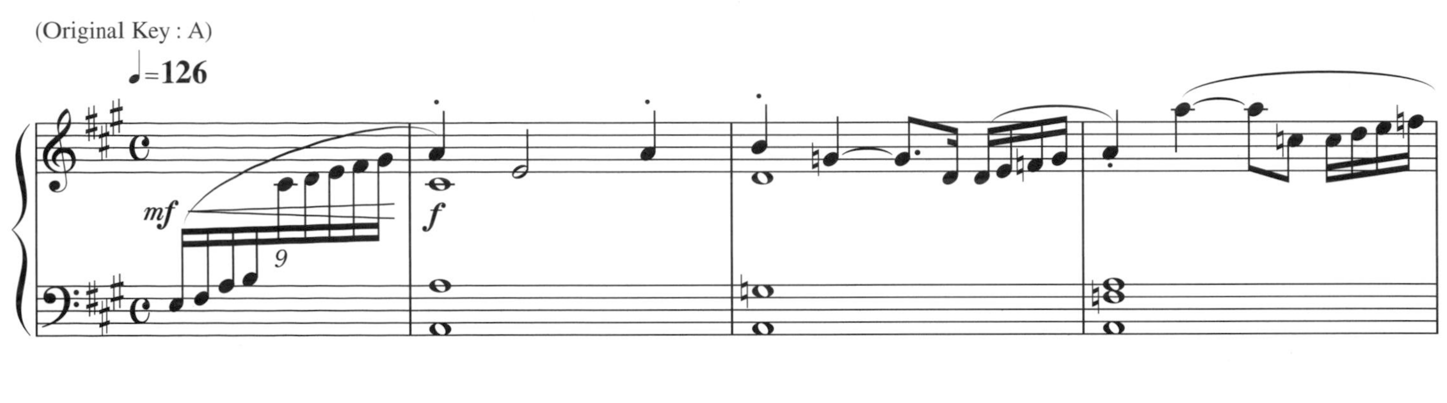

B
mp
mf
f
mp
C
F.O.

THE LEGEND OF ZELDA™: Spirit Tracks
FIELD THEME

Piano arrangement by SHINOBU AMAYAKE
Music supervision by NINTENDO

Composed by MANAKA TOMINAGA

(Original Key : C♯m)

B
mp
C
mf
D
f
E
mf
F.O.

THE LEGEND OF ZELDA™: Spirit Tracks
TRAIN TRAVEL (MAIN THEME)

Piano arrangement by SHINOBU AMAYAKE
Music supervision by NINTENDO

Composed by TORU MINEGISHI

(Original Key : Em)

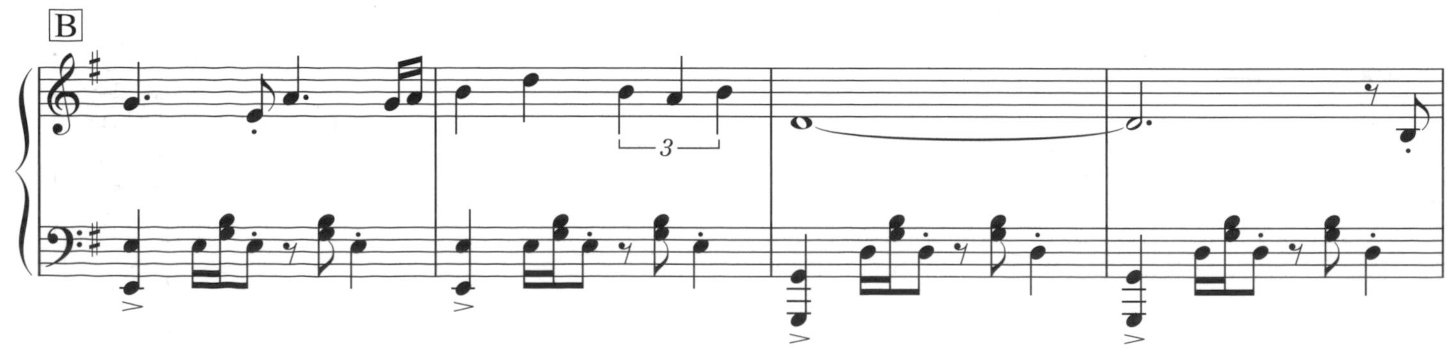

C
3
f
D
3
3
3

E
3
mp
1.
2.
mf
F
3
mp
3
3

G
3
3
mf
3
f
H
mf
D.S.&F.O.

THE LEGEND OF ZELDA™:
TRI-FORCE FANFARE

Composed by TORU MINEGISHI
Piano arrangement by SHINOBU AMAYAKE
Music supervision by NINTENDO

(Original Key : G)

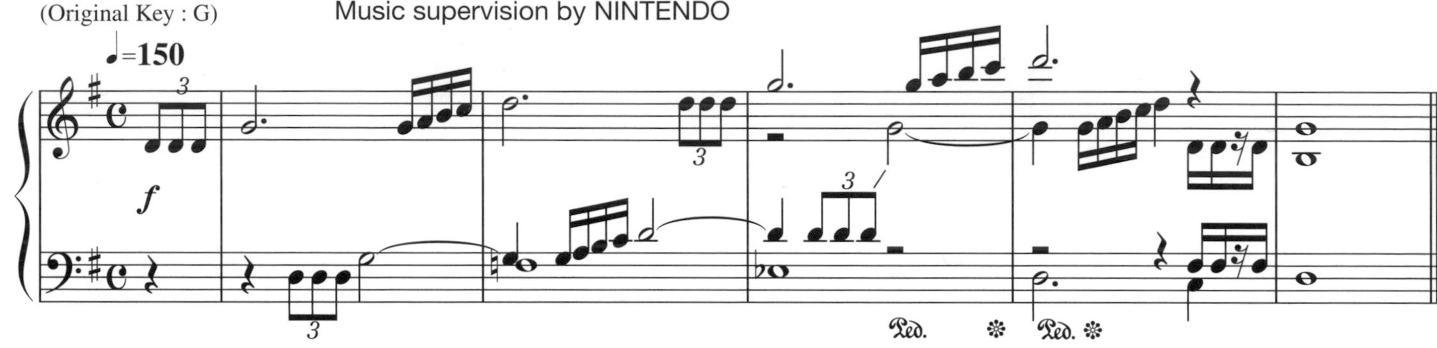

THE LEGEND OF ZELDA™:
CORRECT SOLUTION

(Original Key : C)

Composed by TORU MINEGISHI
Piano arrangement by SHINOBU AMAYAKE
Music supervision by NINTENDO

THE LEGEND OF ZELDA™:
WHISTLE OF WARP

Composed by TORU MINEGISHI
Piano arrangement by SHINOBU AMAYAKE
Music supervision by NINTENDO